Erika Åberg

Modern Knits from Sweden

A warm mix of shawls, scarves, cowls, mittens, hats and more

Photography:
Malin Nuhma

TRAFALGAR SQUARE
North Pomfret, Vermont

First published in the United States
of America
in 2016 by
Trafalgar Square Books
North Pomfret, Vermont 05053

Originally published in Swedish as
Sticka sjalar.

Copyright © 2015 Erika Åberg and
Bokförlaget Semic
English translation © 2016 Trafalgar
Square Books

ISBN: 978-1-57076-782-1

Library of Congress Control
Number: 2016943089

Photography: Malin Nuhma
Charts: Heléne Wallin
Interior Layout: Anja Larsson
Editor: Eva Bergman
Translator: Carol Huebscher
Rhoades

Printed in Malaysia

10 9 8 7 6 5 4 3 2 1

CONTENTS

PREFACE

To knit for yourself and for others is to give yourself time—time, and the opportunity to think, be, and learn. It might sound a little clichéd, but it's so worthwhile to be *present* in every stitch, especially in knitting that requires concentration and close attention. Feeling the material against your skin and teaching your hands to work with the needles is both calming and challenging. Challenging because when you're knitting you have to make decisions—plan, think, and reconsider; calming because of the repetitive movement from stitch to stitch. And in the end you get twice as much out of it: I can knit myself into a quiet mood, and at the same time I'm creating something beautiful and useful, with nothing but yarn and my own imagination. The more knowledge I have, the more closely the end result will match the design I have in mind when I begin.

The following pages hold a collection of garments—shawls, scarves, cowls, and other accessories—I hope you will like, both decorative and useful. I've also tried to find a good balance between garter stitch designs that just lope along and projects to challenge you with something interesting you'll want to use again. Perhaps you will learn something new—about knitting, materials, traditions, or maybe even about yourself. My hope is that you'll really love knitting with your own hands, and will be inspired to discover new materials and yarns and to teach yourself more. Knit all kinds of things that will fit you, warm you, keep you comfortable, and above all, make you happy.

And never forget how nice it is to knit with others! Really, that's about as good as it gets.

Erika Åberg

SHAWLS

If there's one thing I use every single day all year round, it's a shawl. Shawls are not always knitted, but many are. Shawls, scarves, cowls, and snoods are like jewelry that can keep you warm! Whether it's a large square shawl in the Shetland lace tradition, a striped garter stitch snood in the softest wool, or a cowl with a graphic pattern in several colors, I feel like I'm wearing something that's lovely in its own special way. A little tradition, a little history, a little knowledge, and of course a piece of my own knitting. That's the eternal appeal of handmade objects: materials, technique, tradition, and also intention.

It can seem trivial: It's only a scarf, just a pair of half gloves, a simple hat. But everyone who does handwork knows it's more than that. Exacting, done with care, nothing wasted or unnecessary—and even though it is exacting, that doesn't mean it isn't also fun! Knitting is like life: many contradictory things at once.

I have tried to include all kinds of different shapes and styles to wear around your neck. Something for those of you who, like me, prefer to have your arms free and hate having to spend time straightening out the ends of your scarves when bicycling, raking, or pushing the children in the swing; something light and delicate; something thick and comfortable and fun. No matter what you like, there should be something here for you!

This type of garment comes in a variety of shapes. Shawls can be knitted as round, square, rectangular, triangular, a semi-circle, or a mix of everything. You can begin almost anywhere you like—at the far side, at a corner, at the center, or at the top—with thick needles or fine needles, using almost any yarn you like. Choose carefully!

There is plenty of tradition to work with and research for anyone who wants to pursue it. I heartily recommend the textile collections and other resources preserved in museums around the world. Don't forget to visit digital museums! And don't forget that tradition is a living creature that can only grow and thrive through what we make and add. There's also everything to do with fashion and style: When you make a garment yourself, you can freely pick and choose elements from all the different eras of style and beautiful fashions that have come and gone. All the choices you can possibly make might seem dizzying—but always go with your gut feeling. What do you really want to wear?

Think of the projects in this book as the ends of much longer threads, ideas about what a shawl or scarf could be. Use the various colors, shapes, or stitches wherever you want them. And plan things out a little before you begin! Is it important that the garment be nice on both the right and wrong sides? When do you want to wear the garment? If it'll be bothersome to have shawl tips that hang down, maybe a better bet is a cowl, snood, or collar? Play with materials, structures, and shapes!

MATERIALS

I've chosen to knit exclusively with natural materials in this book, partly because I've always loved how they feel against the skin and partly because I'm familiar with them. I know how they behave in all kinds of situations—when I use them, I know I won't be surprised! (It's always fun to try new materials, but sometimes it doesn't work out the way you'd expected ...)

Of course, it depends on what you want in a hand-knitted garment, or for clothes in general. I want garments to be durable in color and shape, and, if I'm lucky enough to still have them, to retain these qualities as they age. It's also important for the process of producing the material to be good for people, animals, and nature. And it's not as important for me to be able to throw the garment into the washing machine after every use. Call me lazy, but I'd rather hang a garment out to air!

I knitted most of the pieces in this book with wool yarn, but there's also a little alpaca, and one linen shawl, too. What are the differences between these materials?

WOOL

Sheep's wool insulates against both heat and cold and is warming even when wet. Wool is also stretchy, particularly when wet, so wool garments should never be hung up after washing—they need to dry flat to prevent them from losing their shape. Wool can absorb moisture twice as well as cotton, which is one of several reasons wool can be very pleasant to wear against your skin.

Each breed of sheep has its own combination of wool types and qualities. Fleeces generally consist of three types of fiber: outer coat (hair), undercoat (wool), and kemp (short, very coarse hair). The balance between these types of fiber will determine what that fleece will be suitable for. Wool (the undercoat) is soft, short, and crimpy. These fibers are closest to the sheep's body and keep it warm, but don't repel moisture very well. The outer coat of hair covering the wool is thick, wavy, and has more strength. These fibers are lustrous and shed water. Kemp is usually only found on the most primitive sheep these days, and is hollow, coarse, and breaks easily. However, kemp can also be pretty, especially when the fleece is dyed, because the kemp doesn't take up dye the same way other fibers do. Wool's water resistance comes from a fat called lanolin, which gives wool a characteristic smell and is another of wool's good qualities.

Wool can, if it is not processed, be felted—this can be good or bad, depending on what you want. With some knowledge, you can felt a piece so the stitches will cohere, and you can shape the fabric and get what you want when you want. If you'd rather your garment didn't felt, processed wool is coated with a plastic film (in simple terms); it's still warming, but doesn't have all the positive qualities of unprocessed wool.

ALPACA

Alpacas are camelids that originated in the Andes: Peru, Bolivia, and Chile. There are basically two types of alpaca: Huacaya and Suri. Their fiber is lustrous, fine, and very, very soft. In general, alpaca fiber is drier and silkier than wool, because alpacas don't produce lanolin and because the individual fibers are usually finer than the fibers that make up sheep's wool. Even here, though, there are big variations. Some people who are allergic to wool can wear alpaca without itching or being irritated. Alpaca fiber is typically warmer than sheep's wool, too—it has microscopic "pockets" in its fibers that are full of insulating air. Some people find alpaca *too* warm, though, and in that case it's a good idea to blend alpaca with sheep's wool or silk. That way you can enjoy the good qualities of several fibers all at once.

A sojourn in Boge.
At the house of Birgitta Rasmussan and Benny Dandahl on the northeast part of the island of Gotland, we were able to greet and photograph alpacas, sheep, and lambs. They have a little farm with Huacaya alpacas and Leicester and Gotland sheep, as well as pygmy goats and a well regarded dog kennel.

LINEN

Linen is a plant fiber that comes from flax, and is produced with very little or no environmental impact, particularly in comparison with cotton. Flax has long, smooth fibers and is lustrous and strong. It can withstand stress when both wet and dry, which is one of the many reasons it's used so often for textiles. However, it's not as flexible as wool, which is why it wrinkles so easily. It's also easy for air to pass through linen, which means it tends to let warmth escape and thus typically makes garments cooler than wool or cotton. Linen fiber tolerates heat better than synthetic fibers and bleaches quickly in comparison with cotton. Linen garments tend to grow softer and more lustrous over time. It's easy to learn more about flax processing from the field to the finished linen fiber—and very exciting!

I hope you're interested in understanding your materials and choosing them carefully. Try different materials and compare. Perhaps you'll even learn to spin! Following your materials all the way from the very beginning in the field or garden to becoming a yarn, and then transforming it into a garment stitch by stitch is an unbeatable experience. Today there are many good opportunities to try spinning—maybe even where you live?

For anyone who wants to deepen their knowledge and learn more about materials, there are several suggestions for resources at the back of this book. There is so much to learn!

BLOCKING AND GARMENT CARE

If you take care of your clothing, it'll last longer. A wool garment is at its best when worn. If you want it to last, it's a good idea to air out the garment regularly. Shake it out or brush it off between airings. By doing so, you can also ensure that unwelcome guests won't eat your favorite garments. Don't let your clothing hang too long—that can cause the fibers to tear and the garment will lose its shape. Also, do not leave your garments out in direct sunlight. If you air out your garments often, particularly those made of wool and alpaca, do so in humid weather.

There's nothing wrong with mending most garments, and it honestly doesn't matter very much if the darning shows a little bit. It doesn't hurt to save any yarn remaining after a garment is finished as a little stash of mending yarn—just in case.

Wash garments when necessary, but first clean off any specks with soap (wool-safe, if the garment requires it). When the entire garment needs to be washed, make sure you use the right amount of soap and rinse it out well. Wool fibers react well to acids such as vinegar and white wine vinegar, as do many other animal fibers; but they don't care for alkaloids like lye, which will make the fibers brittle.

Gently wash and rinse wool and alpaca fibers in lukewarm water. It's best to keep the water at 86°F / 30°C. Rapid changes between hot and cold water aren't good for these fibers—that increases the risk of shrinking or felting. If you want to felt something, that's another story. As far as regular washing goes: Never scrub, twist, or wring a garment. Fibers need care when they're wet, and it's easy to ruin their look.

Add a little white or white wine vinegar to the last rinse water to keep animal fibers lustrous.

Linen can be washed at 140°F / 60°C, but don't keep it at that temperature for long. Soak the garment for about 20 minutes before washing. Linen can be washed using the wool setting on your washing machine.

In principle, I would like to warn you away from tumble drying. That applies to linen as well as wool and alpaca. Hanging garments up isn't preferable, either. It's so much better to let a garment dry flat to avoid losing the garment shape!

Once you've washed a garment, you can let it dry as follows: Press the water out of the rinsed garment, but do not wring. Lay the garment on a hand towel. A wool garment needs care, as mentioned before, but it is also flexible and can be shaped when it is wet. Now roll up the towel from the top down, not side to side. Do not wring or press the towel; just let it absorb the excess water gently. When the garment is almost dry, you can roll the towel out and put your piece on another clean, dry towel. Pat out the garment to finished measurements and leave to dry completely on the towel.

Maybe the garment needs more blocking to achieve the right size or shape? Pin it out to the desired size and shape on an ironing board or another surface. Don't be stingy with the pins!

To learn more about wool, linen, and other textile materials, read "Materials" on page 15 and also look at the Resources section on page 107.

Half Gloves

READ BEFORE YOU KNIT

Even if many of the patterns are simple, this is not a book about knitting basics. If you need a book about the basics, check the Resources page at this back of this book for recommendations. No matter how experienced a knitter you are, it's always a good idea to have a comprehensive book about the fundamentals so you can look up information when you are trying something new or want an alternate method. There's always something new to learn!

Read through the entire pattern before you start knitting. It's always good to have an idea about what you're going to need to do during each part of a pattern. If there are different instructions for different sizes, you need to be careful and follow the same set of instructions throughout.

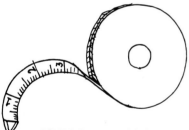

EQUIPMENT AND TOOLS

Choosing your main tools, your knitting needles, can be easy as pie or need a lot of knowledge. Either use what you have on hand or try out the various styles of needles on the market. Maybe you'll find several favorites.

I think needles should be sharp-pointed—preferably with a long point. Stubby needles don't work well for me at all. Keep in mind that wooden needles need to be used for a while before they'll get nice and smooth; they may snag the yarn now and then in the beginning, but are often worth the trouble.

Pretty much all the time—when the knitting doesn't specifically require double-pointed needles—I like to knit with a circular needle, even when knitting back and forth. That way, I can knit with my elbows next to my body and work more ergonomically; it also makes it easier to take my knitting with me.

Although the needle points are important, they're not the only thing that matters! The join between the needle and the cable on a circular must be smooth. When choosing a circular, check it carefully. Make sure there are no notches, gaps, or unintended hooks or bends. If there are, those needles should be put away. You'll only get frustrated with them, and you should save all your patience for complicated patterns.

It is actually remarkable how much easier it is to accomplish and enjoy all sorts of creative work when the materials, tools, and creator work together. Find the combination that works best for you, and let it take some time.

This doesn't mean that you should throw away all the needles you've bought or perhaps inherited. Go through them, bundle the sets of double-points, and arrange them so they are at the ready. Inventory all your needles. They'll be your best friends.

What else do you need? A measuring tape; a pair of small, sharp scissors; and pins to block your garments. It's also good to have sewing needles handy for sewing up seams and weaving in yarn ends. You should probably make sure you own both a finer embroidery needle without a point and a bigger large-eye needle.

SWATCHES AND GAUGE

I know, it's old news for many of us: but gauge is actually very important and that needs to be repeated. It's so very disappointing when you don't realize how worthwhile a gauge swatch would have been until you've already finished a garment. Many knitters can attest to how easy it is to just

start knitting—and how crestfallen they feel when the piece doesn't come out right.

Simply put: Make a gauge swatch with the recommended yarn and needles and check the gauge. Make sure the fabric has the feel you want. Measure your swatch and decide whether the needles are okay or you need to choose a different size.

The gauge is what you need to match so you can knit the piece as desired. By choosing needles that, in your hands, allow you to match the recommended number of stitches per inch/centimeter exactly, or at least as closely as possible, you can be sure the garment will achieve the measurements and proportions you want. Of course, you can choose to work without a gauge—but you need to pay very close attention so you can control the process at every stage and reach the desired end result.

YARN CHOICE AND YARN SIZES

Many yarns come wrapped with a band (the ball band) that gives you, the knitter, important information. It might list the fiber content and total length, and it should tell you if the yarn has been processed a certain way and is or isn't washable. Some yarn mills also list the recommended gauge for knitting.

I have chosen some of my favorite yarns for the projects in this book. If you can't find the exact same yarns, or maybe want to knit with yarns you already have at home, it's a good idea to check the yarn size.

Sometime the yarn size is listed as a pair of numbers, like "6/2," "8/2," "8/1," or something similar. This method of sizing yarn is very common in Sweden and something you're more likely to see if you have access to older yarn. It's not self-explanatory, but it is very logical and smart once you understand the system.

The information given with these numbers indicates how many meters are in a kilo. A 6/2 wool yarn is a two-ply yarn with each strand at 6,000 meters per kilo (m/kg). When the two strands are plied together, the yarn then has 3,000 m/kg. An 8/2 wool yarn is thinner, with 4,000 m/kg or 400 m / 100 g skein.

If you choose another size of yarn, the garment will simply be a different size. It doesn't take much to change the size of a garment without also having to recalculate the numbers in the instructions. When you make these types of changes, it's important to maintain the desired proportions.

SPLICING YARNS

The nice thing about knitting with pure, untreated wool yarn is that you can easily splice two strands of yarn together when you change to a new skein. Do not cut the yarn ends; just untwist them for an inch or so / 2-3 cm, fluff out the ends, and overlap the ends in your palm. Spit (gently!) on the overlapping ends and rub the yarn vigorously between your palms. Saliva and friction will felt the ends together and then you can continue right on knitting.

SEAMING

Use a blunt-tipped tapestry needle for sewing up. A thick needle will easily work between the stitches and around the strands without splitting the yarn. Finishing without splitting the yarn will make things easier for you later, if you need to undo a garment, undo the bind-off to make it longer or shorter, or simply want to rip the whole thing out and use the yarn elsewhere.

FINISHING

Begin by weaving in all the yarn ends. Sew a few

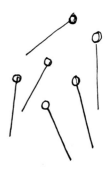

stitches as invisibly as possible on the wrong side to help conceal the end, and then trim, leaving a short end on the wrong side. Be careful—if you trim the ends too short, there is a good chance that those ends will pop out on to the right side of the piece.

Now the garment should be wet-blocked. Soak the piece in lukewarm water and then roll it in a towel and press out the excess water. If you can get your washing machine to cooperate, you can spin the water out. Lay the garment flat on a towel and leave until completely dry. Don't be afraid to shape and pat the garment to finished measurements while it is still damp.

If you've knitted a lace piece, you need to block it so the pattern will be clearly visible. Carefully block the damp piece so the pattern stands out and the piece reaches the correct measurements. You may need to pin the piece into the right shape and size and then leave to dry completely.

A FEW BASIC TERMS

Garter Stitch Stripes
Many designs use garter stitch in which every row is knitted. Garter ridge is a well-known term and a way to keep control and count of the rows. A garter ridge = two rows of knitting; together they form a garter stripe or ridge and make it easier to count the rows in garter stitch.

Increasing a Stitch
Many knitters have their own favorite way of increasing a stitch. In the pattern for the half gloves in this book on page 42 and later on page 81, I wanted the increased stitch to be as invisible as possible. I picked up the strand between two stitches of the previous row (use left needle tip to lift strand from front to back), and knit into it through the back loop. This prevents the strand from becoming a yarnover, which would make a hole. On the next row, be extra careful when you come to this new stitch. On the other hand, as for both triangular shawls, the increased stitches *are*

yarnovers, which was done on purpose to make them decorative.

Edge Stitches
The way a knitter works edge stitches is simply a matter of taste, particularly when it comes to the method for making the first stitch of every row. Naturally, it depends on whether or not the garment will be joined with another type of edging or if the edging needs to be firm or look good. Decide on your own favorite method. I usually slip the first stitch purlwise, but for some projects, I purl the first stitch instead. Try out various methods and see how each looks and functions.

ABBREVIATIONS

BO	bind off (= British cast off)	mm	millimeter(s)
		p	purl
CC	contrast color	p2tog	purl 2 stitches together = 1 st decreased
cm	centimeter(s)		
CO	cast on	pm	place marker
dpn	double-pointed needled	psso	pass slipped st(s) over
k	knit	rem	remain(s)(ing)
k2tog	knit 2 stitches together = 1 st decreased; right-leaning decrease	RLI	right lifted increase—knit into right side of st below
kfb	knit into front and then back of same stitch = 1 st increased	rnd(s)	round(s)
		RS	right side
		sl	slip
LLI	left lifted increase—knit into left side of st below	slm	slip marker
		ssk	slip, slip, knit—(sl next st knitwise) 2 times; knit into back loops = 1 st decreased; left-leaning decrease
M1	make 1—with left needle tip, lift strand between two stitches from front to back and knit into back loop		
		st(s)	stitch(es)
		tbl	through back loop(s)
m	meter(s)	WS	wrong side
MC	main color	yd	yard(s)
		yo	yarnover

ZIGZAG COWL

A soft and very practical cowl knitted with four colors in two color sections. The pattern is simple and you can easily vary the overall look by blending in several colors at shorter intervals. I knitted this cowl with two colorways to lighten it up a bit. It's a little like the sea and sky here on Gotland on a clear and cold winter day, with white geese on the waves and puffy clouds spread over a light blue sky. A true favorite!

FINISHED MEASUREMENTS:
6¾ x 64½ in / 17 x 164 cm

MATERIALS: CYCA #2 (sport/baby) Visjö from Östergötlands Ullspinneri (100% wool, 328 yd/ 300 m / 100 g)

COLORS: Dark Blue, Light Gray, Sky Blue, White

YARN AMOUNTS: 100 g each of Dark Blue and Light Gray; 40 g each of Sky Blue and White

NEEDLES: U.S. size 8 / 5 mm, circular

GAUGE: 28 sts in charted pattern = 4 in / 10 cm.

Adjust needle size to obtain correct gauge if necessary.

- The pattern is a repeat of 6 sts. If you want a wider or narrower cowl, cast on multiples of 6 stitches. One repeat is slightly less than 1¼ in / 3 cm wide. The cowl shown here has 16 repeats, with the last repeat losing the last stitch to join the knitting in the round.
- CO 95 sts. I cast on with two colors, following the first row on the chart. Grit your teeth and it will go well. This cast-on will make it much easier to join the piece when the time comes. Being careful not to twist cast-on row, join; pm at beginning of round. Work in pattern following the chart. The red frame encloses the repeat.
- When the piece is approx. 50 in / 127 cm long, ending with a Row 3 on the chart, change colors so Sky Blue takes the place of Dark Blue and White substitutes for Light Gray. Continue in pattern for another 14½ in / 37 cm. Save a bit of the Dark Blue and Light Gray for the finishing.
- After binding off, finish the cowl. I washed the piece, blocked to the finished measurements, and left it until dry. Join the cowl by twisting the tube one turn and joining the cast-on and bound-off edges as follows:
- This finishing takes a little patience, good lighting, and concentration. I threaded two tapestry needles—one with Dark Blue and the other with Light Gray. I worked in Kitchener stitch to join the ends, matching the colors as in the pattern. It is worth the trouble to seam the piece so the join is almost invisible and very smooth.
- After joining, I gently steam-pressed the seam so the stitches would align well.

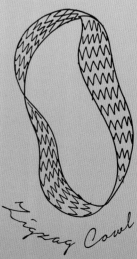

This cowl is knitted as a long tube. It will be very warm because it is doubled. That means you can also knit it somewhat loosely because the doubling will make it feel substantial. Don't knit it too loosely, though, or the pattern won't show well.

PEACOCK SCARF

For this scarf, one of the most classic lace patterns takes on a new form—in another direction. It's a nice and easy lace pattern to begin with, fun and pretty to knit. Sometimes this is called a "sea-shell" pattern and sometimes "peacock." The motif can be found in many parts of the world but it's particularly common in the Shetland Islands.

- Loosely CO 260 sts (= 252 sts for pattern + 4 edge sts at each side). Make sure the edge is not too tight. Begin and end every row with k4 (edge sts). Work 4 rows in garter st.
- Work in lace pattern following the chart. **NOTE:** The edge sts are not shown on the chart.
- **Row 1:** K4 (edge sts), *(k2tog) 3 times, (k1, yo) 6 times, (ssk) 3 times*; repeat from * to * 13 more times and end with k4 (edge sts).
- **Row 2:** Knit across.
- **Row 3:** Knit across.
- **Row 4:** K4, purl to last 4 sts and end with k4.
- Repeat Rows 1–4 until piece is approx. 14½ in / 37 cm long. End with 4 rows garter st (knit all rows) and then BO loosely.
- Weave in all ends neatly on WS and then block (see page 30).

FINISHED MEASUREMENTS: 70½ in / 180 cm long, 15¾ in / 40 cm wide

MATERIALS: CYCA #4 (worsted/afghan/aran) Ullgarn Extra 2 from Yllet (95% wool/5% Merino wool, 219 yd/200 m / 100 g)

YARN AMOUNT AND COLOR: 250 g Petroleum Green 363

NEEDLES: U.S. size 9 / 5.5 mm: 60 in / 150 cm long circular

GAUGE: 18 sts in charted pattern (= one pattern repeat) = approx. 5¼ in / 13 cm.

Adjust needle size to obtain correct gauge if necessary.

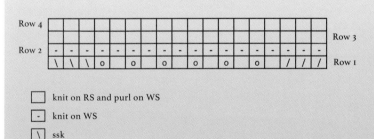

☐ knit on RS and purl on WS

− knit on WS

\\ ssk

o yo

/ k2tog

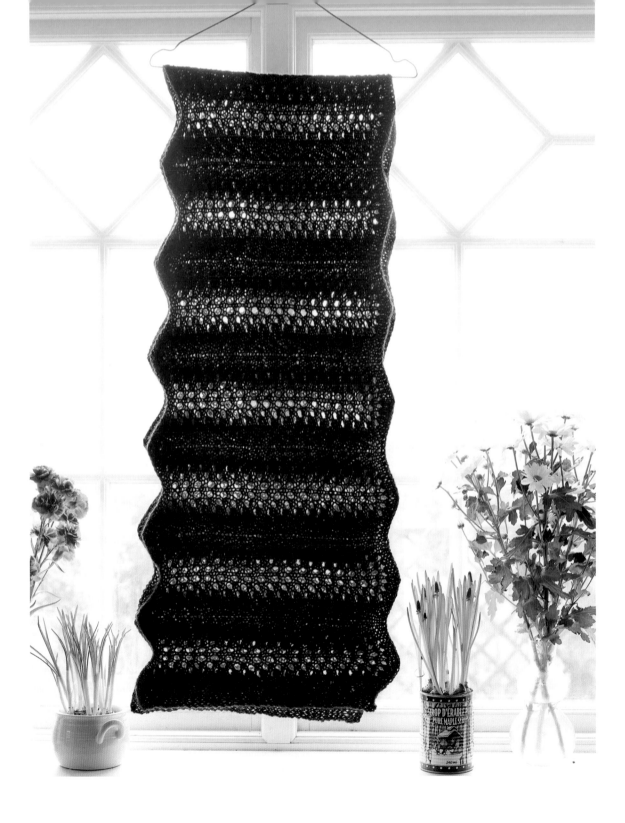

Arrow Scarf

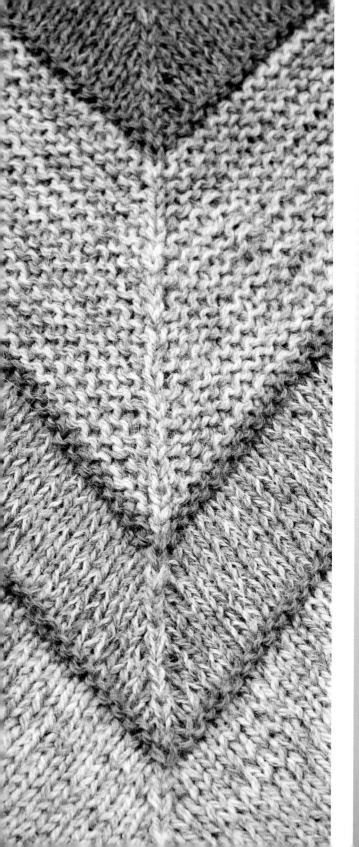

ARROW SCARF

Really, this is just a striped scarf, but stripes can be so many other things. This scarf is shaped like an arrow and the stripes have different structures. Combining these yarns—the soft and light wool with the fine alpaca for a rather thin fabric—brings out the best of each. These are two of my favorite yarns, and this is a scarf I know I'll wear for a long time.

Keep an eye out as you knit with the two strands together. It's easy to catch only one strand.

FINISHED MEASUREMENTS: 11 in / 28 cm wide, 69 in / 175 cm long as measured down center stitch

MATERIALS: CYCA #1 (sock/fingering/baby) Highland Wool from Isager (100% wool, 306 yd/280 m / 50 g) and CYCA #0 (lace/fingering) Alpaca 1 from Isager (100% alpaca, 437 yd/ 400 m / 50 g)

YARN AMOUNTS AND COLORS: Highland Wool: 100 g Sand, 100 g Brown, 50 g Oak, 20 g Rose, 20 g Curry

ALPACA 1: 100 g #7, 20 g #61, 20 g #3, 20 g #59

NEEDLES: U.S. size 6 / 4 mm

GAUGE: 20 sts in stockinette with 1 strand of each yarn held together = 4 in / 10 cm.

Adjust needle size to obtain correct gauge if necessary.

SPECIAL ABBREVIATIONS: HW = Highland Wool; A1 = Alpaca 1

- With one strand HW Sand and one strand A1 #7 held together, CO 51 sts. Working back and forth, knit 5 rows.
- **NOTE:** Throughout, always knit the outermost 4 sts at each side as edge stitches.
- Pm on each side of the 3 center sts.
- Every RS row is an increase/decrease row. The increases are made in the first st inside the edge sts at each side. Decreases are worked in the center of the scarf. Take all measurements for the pattern down the center stitch.
- A stockinette row on RS is worked as follows: K4 (edge sts), k1fb (= 1 st increased), k19, slm, double dec = sl 2 sts knitwise at the same time, k1 and psso (= 2 sts decreased), slm, k19, kfb (= 1 st increased), k4 (edge sts).
- On the next and all following WS rows (except where noted for garter stitch): K4, purl to last 4 sts, end k4.
- **NOTE:** The center stitch is always purled on the WS, even in garter stitch sections.
- **Garter Stitch Ridge:** RS, knit in pattern with increases and decreases; WS, knit across except for center st which is always purled. 2 rows = 1 garter ridge.
- The color sequence for the scarf is listed below. Always change color at the beginning of a RS row.
- 8 in / 20 cm stockinette with HW Sand + A1 #7.
- 1 garter stitch ridge: HW Curry + A1 #3.
- 11 garter ridges with HW Oak + A1 #7.
- 1 garter ridge with HW Curry + A1 #3.
- 2½ in / 6 cm stockinette with HW Sand + A1 #59.
- 1 garter ridge with HW Curry + A1 #3.
- 8 in / 20 cm stockinette with HW Brown + A1 #7.
- 1 garter ridge with HW Curry + A1 #3.
- 11 garter ridges with HW Sand + A1 #7.
- 1 garter ridge with HW Curry + A1 #3.
- 2½ in / 6 cm stockinette with HW Rose + A1 #61.
- 1 garter ridge with HW Curry + A1 #3.
- 8 in / 20 cm stockinette with HW Sand + A1 #7.
- 1 garter ridge with HW Curry + A1 #3.
- 11 garter ridges with HW Oak + A1 #7.
- 1 garter ridge with HW Curry + A1 #3.
- 2½ in / 6 cm stockinette with HW Sand + A1 #59.
- 1 garter ridge with HW Curry + A1 #3.
- 8 in / 20 cm stockinette with HW Brown + A1 #7.
- 1 garter ridge with HW Curry + A1 #3.
- 11 garter ridges with HW Sand + A1 #7.
- 1 garter ridge with HW Curry + A1 #3.
- 2½ in / 6 cm stockinette with HW Rose + A1 #61.
- 1 garter ridge with HW Curry + A1 #3.
- 8 in / 20 cm stockinette with HW Sand + A1 #7.
- Knit 5 rows in garter st with HW Sand and A1 #7. BO loosely (to match tension of cast-on row).
- Weave in all ends neatly on WS. Block (see page 30).

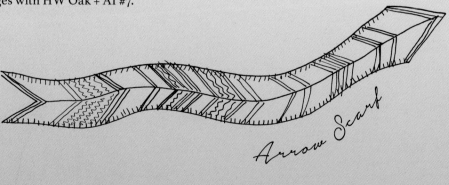

Arrow Scarf

WRIST WARMERS WITH PICOT EDGINGS

I really like half gloves and wrist warmers. They leave my fingers free, and if I am still cold I can put on a pair of mittens over them. These are warm, soft, and practical, especially when I'm wearing a garment with three-quarter length sleeves. The ribbed portion can stretch up your arm for extra warmth or be turned down near the wrist. A warming ornament with a little picot edging.

SIZE: Adult

FINISHED MEASUREMENTS: 18¼ in / 46 cm long; 4¼ in / 11 cm from end of ribbing to picot edging; 3½ in / 9 cm wide, not including thumb gusset; 2½ in / 6 cm from base of thumb to edge of picot edging.

MATERIALS: CYCA #0 (lace/fingering) Ullgarn Extra 1 from Yllet (100% wool–blend of Gotland pälsull and Falkland Merino, 437 yd/400 m / 100 g)

YARN AMOUNT AND COLOR: 70 g Dark Gray 192

NEEDLES: U.S. sizes 0 and 2.5 / 2 and 3 mm, set of 5 dpn

GAUGE: 28 sts in stockinette with smaller needles = 4 in / 10 cm.

Adjust needle sizes to obtain correct gauge if necessary.

YOU'LL ALSO NEED: A needle and contrasting thread or a stitch holder for thumb gusset stitches.

Right-Hand Wrist Warmer
- With larger needles, CO 45 sts; join, being careful not to twist cast-on row. Pm for beginning of rnd. Divide sts as follows:
- Place 10 sts on Ndl 1; 10 sts on Ndl 2, 12 sts on Ndl 3; 13 sts on Ndl 4. Work around in k3, p2 ribbing for 13¾ in / 35 cm. Now slide the sts from Ndl 4 to Ndl 3 and slip the first st on Ndl 3 to Ndl 2 so you have 24 sts on Ndl 3. Change to smaller needles.
- Work in stockinette on Ndls 1 and 2 and in horseshoe pattern on Ndl 3 (see chart on page 44). *At the same time*, begin thumb gusset at beginning of Ndl 1: *RLI, k3, LLI. Work 2 rnds without increasing.* Repeat from * to * for thumb gusset, with 2 more sts between increase sts until there are 13 sts for gusset. Work 2 rnds (or to crook of thumb) and then place the 13 gusset sts on a holder.
- CO 3 sts over gap and continue with stockinette on palm and horseshoe pattern on back of hand until piece is 4¼ in / 11 cm from the top of the ribbing.
- Knit 3 rnds over all sts.
- Finish with a picot edging. Work an eyelet rnd: (Yo, k2tog) around
- Knit 3 rnds.
- BO. Fold edging at eyelet rnd and sew down bound-off edge on WS.
- **Thumb:** Pick up and knit sts as indicated below; Ndl 1 will hold the sts from thumb gusset.
- **Ndl 1:** The 5 sts in the center of the 13 thumb gusset sts on holder
- **Ndl 2:** The next 4 sts of the 13 thumb gusset sts from holder + pick up and knit 2 sts at side of thumbhole = 6 sts total.

>

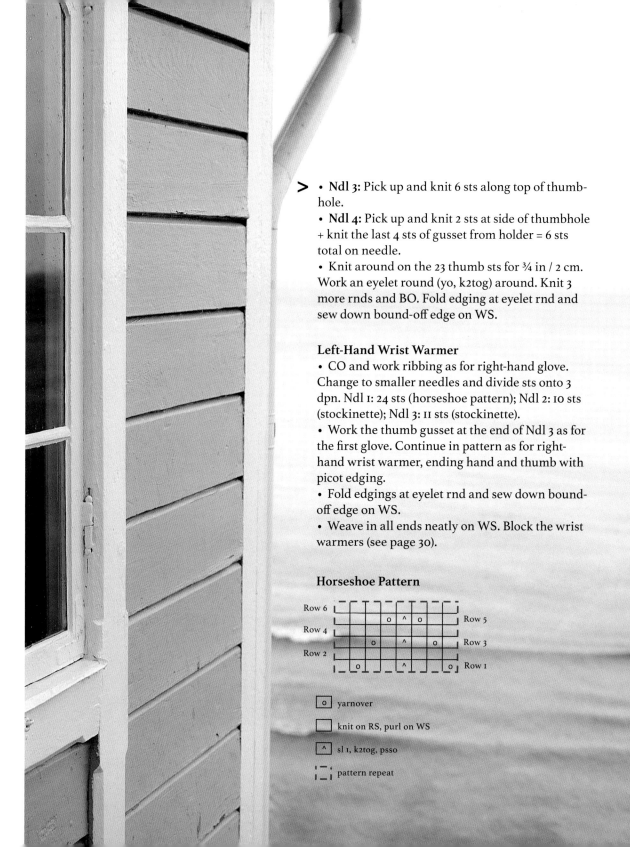

> • **Ndl 3:** Pick up and knit 6 sts along top of thumb-hole.
> • **Ndl 4:** Pick up and knit 2 sts at side of thumbhole + knit the last 4 sts of gusset from holder = 6 sts total on needle.
> • Knit around on the 23 thumb sts for ¾ in / 2 cm. Work an eyelet round (yo, k2tog) around. Knit 3 more rnds and BO. Fold edging at eyelet rnd and sew down bound-off edge on WS.

Left-Hand Wrist Warmer

• CO and work ribbing as for right-hand glove. Change to smaller needles and divide sts onto 3 dpn. Ndl 1: 24 sts (horseshoe pattern); Ndl 2: 10 sts (stockinette); Ndl 3: 11 sts (stockinette).

• Work the thumb gusset at the end of Ndl 3 as for the first glove. Continue in pattern as for right-hand wrist warmer, ending hand and thumb with picot edging.

• Fold edgings at eyelet rnd and sew down bound-off edge on WS.

• Weave in all ends neatly on WS. Block the wrist warmers (see page 30).

Horseshoe Pattern

Row 6
Row 5
Row 4
Row 3
Row 2
Row 1

| o | yarnover |

| | knit on RS, purl on WS |

| ^ | sl 1, k2tog, psso |

| - - | pattern repeat |

HERRINGBONE SCARF

Here's a good basic scarf that suits everyone. The yarn is soft and easy to knit with; just make sure that your needles don't split it. The technique is simple but very effective, making a rather compact fabric. When working in herringbone, always choose a larger size needle than usual for the yarn.

- With Natural White, CO 36 sts with an elastic cast-on method (for example, a knitted or cable CO).
- **Row 1 (WS):** Purl across.
- **Row 2 (RS):** K1 (edge st), *k2tog through back loops, slipping only the first st from the left needle*. Repeat from * to * until 2 sts rem and end with k2.
- **Row 3 (WS):** K1 (edge st), *p2tog, slipping only the first st from the left needle*. Repeat from * to * until 2 sts rem and end with p1, k1 (edge st).
- Repeat Rows 2–3. Continue in pattern until you've used up both skeins of Natural White. Change to Brown-Gray and continue until you have only enough yarn to bind off. BO loosely.
- Weave in all ends neatly on WS. Block scarf (see page 30), or, if you prefer, place the scarf between two damp pressing cloths and steam-press on wrong side.

FINISHED MEASUREMENTS:
8 in / 20 cm wide; 65 in / 165 cm long

MATERIALS: CYCA #4 (worsted/afghan/aran) Marks & Kattens Eco Ull (80% wool, 20% Merino wool, 90 yd / 82 m / 50 g)

YARN AMOUNTS AND COLORS:
100 g (2 skeins) each of Natural White 1980 and Brown-Gray 1982

NEEDLES: U.S. size 15 / 10 mm

GAUGE: 17 sts in pattern = 4 in / 10 cm.

Adjust needle size to obtain correct gauge if necessary.

Herringbone Scarf

LINEN SHAWL

A slightly heavy linen shawl with a fine drape and an easy edging. The shawl is worked from the top down with two strands of yarn held together. That way, you avoid casting on many stitches and the stitches and stripes will form a pretty V-shape. You can knit this shawl with one color, a big assortment of random colors, or stripes of garter stitch and stockinette.

FINISHED MEASUREMENTS: 22 in / 56 cm from center st at top down to bottom lace tip; 56¼ in / 143 cm across top edge, not including lace edging

MATERIALS: CYCA #3 (DK/ light worsted) Lin from Yllet (100% linen, 240 yd/219 m / 100 g)

YARN AMOUNTS AND COLORS: 200 g Unbleached 2001 (MC); 100 g Light Pink 2086 (CC1) for body of shawl; approx. 25 g Red 2074 (CC2) for edging

NEEDLES: U.S. size 8 / 5 mm for body of shawl; U.S. size 6 / 4 mm for lace edging

GAUGE: 14 sts in garter st with 2 strands held together on larger needles = 4 in / 10 cm.

Adjust needle size to obtain correct gauge if necessary.

- This shawl is worked in garter st (knit all rows) with 2 strands of yarn held together throughout.
- **NOTE:** Always slip the first st of every row purlwise. A garter ridge = 2 knit rows.
With MC, CO 7 sts.
- **Row 1:** Knit across = 2 edge sts at each side and 3 center sts. Pm before and after these 3 center sts.
- **Row 2:** K2 (edge sts), yo, k3 (center sts), yo, k2 (edge sts).
- **Row 3:** Knit. Continue knitting every row, working increases on even-numbered rows.
- **Row 4:** K2, yo, knit to first marker, yo, slm, k3, slm, yo, knit until 2 sts rem, yo, k2. The increases will always be inside each of the 2 edge sts at each side and on each side of the narrow k-3 panel at center.
- Repeat Rows 3–4, working color sequence as suggested below.
- 14 garter ridges MC; 3 ridges CC1, (6 ridges MC, 3 ridges CC1) approx. 4 times. The first MC section is wider than subsequent sections.
- I used CC2 to bind off the sts following last CC1 row. Use an elastic bind-off as described below.
- This bind-off method works well any time you need a stretchy edge. K2, *slip the 2 sts from right ndl back to left ndl and knit the 2 sts together through back loops. Now there is 1 st on right ndl. Knit 1 st and repeat from * across.
- Now you can knit the edging if you like. Work with 2 strands of CC2 held together and smaller needles. For lace edging pattern, see page 88.
- Weave in all ends neatly on WS. Block shawl (see page 30).

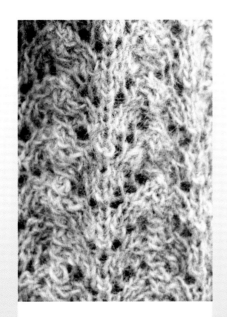

HORSESHOE SHAWL

A very long, rather open lace shawl in the softest wool. I made my shawl a little longer than my height. This is a favorite for both everyday wear and parties!

- The shawl has 8 repeats of the pattern across. Each repeat has 8 sts. Add or subtract repeats to make the shawl wider or narrower.
- CO 64 sts and knit 4 rows.
- With 4 edge sts at each side (knit edge sts on every row), work in charted pattern below.
- **NOTE:** If you want a fine and uniform edging, always slip the first st of every row purlwise.
- Work in Horseshoe pattern following the chart.
- When piece is approx. 73⅝ in / 187 cm long, end with Row 6 of chart and then knit 4 rows. BO loosely. Weave in all ends neatly on WS. Block shawl (see page 30).

FINISHED MEASUREMENTS: 14¼ in / 36 cm long; 74¾ in / 190 cm long

MATERIALS: CYCA #0 (lace/ fingering) Ullgarn Extra 1 from Yllet (100% wool–blend of Gotland pälsull and Falkland Merino, 437 yd/ 400 m / 100 g)

YARN AMOUNT AND COLOR: 175 g Light Gray 196

NEEDLES: U.S. size 6 / 4 mm

GAUGE: 1 repeat of 8 sts in charted pattern is a little less than 2 in / 5 cm wide when slightly stretched.

Adjust needle size to obtain correct gauge if necessary.

Horseshoe Pattern

The chart shows all rows.
Odd-numbered rows = RS;
even-numbered rows = WS.

o yarnover

☐ knit on RS, purl on WS

^ sl 1, k2tog, psso

pattern repeat

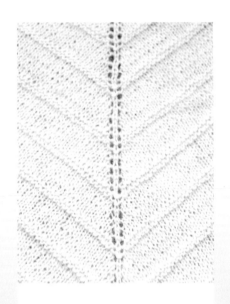

SMALL WHITE BASIC SHAWL

The world's easiest, prettiest, and lightest basic pattern for a triangular shawl—with endless possibilities for variation. The heavy linen shawl on page 49 is worked on the same principles. For this example, I knitted a fine but firm shawl just big enough to tie around your neck inside your coat. Choose a different yarn and bigger needles and you'll get a completely different result.

FINISHED MEASUREMENTS: 23¾ in / 60 cm from center st at top down to bottom lace tip; 51¼ in / 130 cm across top edge

MATERIALS: CYCA #1 (sock/fingering/baby) 1 ply yarn from Solkustens Spinnverkstad (100% wool, 459 yd/420 m / 100 g)

YARN AMOUNT AND COLOR: 100 g White

NEEDLES: U.S. size 2.5 / 3 mm

GAUGE: 22 sts in stockinette = 4 in / 10 cm.

Adjust needle size to obtain correct gauge if necessary.

- CO 5 sts = 2 edge sts at each side and 1 center st. Pm at each side of center st and slip markers as you come to them. Always purl the first st and work the rem sts across as specified in pattern. On every RS row, you will increase 4 sts.
- Increase with yo on each side of the center st and inside the edge sts at each side.
- **Row 1:** P1, k1 (edge sts), yo, k1 (center st), yo, k2 (edge sts).
- **Row 2:** P1, k1, p3, k2.
- **Row 3:** P1, k1, yo, k1, yo, k1, yo, k1, yo, k2.
- **Row 4:** P1, k1, p7, k2.
- **Row 5:** P1, k1, yo, k3, yo, k1, yo, k3, yo, k2.
- **Row 6:** P1, k1, p11, k2.
- **Row 7:** P1, k1, yo, k5, yo, k1, yo, k5 yo, k2.
- **Row 8:** P1, k1, p15, k2.
- **Row 9:** P1, k1, yo, k7, yo, k1, yo, k7 yo, k2.
- **Row 10:** P1, k1, p19, k2.
- **Row 11:** P1, k1, yo, k9, yo, k1, yo, k9 yo, k2.
- **Row 12:** P1, k1, p23, k2.
- Continue as set, increasing on every odd-numbered row. Work 9 rows in stockinette and then knit 3 rows, with the first of the 3 knit rows on the WS. Repeat this sequence 12 times for a total of 13 repeats of 9 + 3 rows. On the final repeat, work as follows: 9 rows stockinette + 2 knit rows.
- BO on WS as follows: K2, *slip the 2 sts from right ndl back to left ndl and knit the 2 sts together through back loops. Now there is 1 st on right ndl. Knit 1 st and repeat from * across. This method makes a stretchy and decorative edge.
- Weave in all ends neatly on WS. Block shawl (see page 30).

BEAR HAT

A warm, soft hat and cowl combined—with ears. It couldn't be any sweeter! This hat's quick to knit and will fit children 1–3 years old. If you want a larger size, you can add a few stitches and rows. There are 11 stitches to 4 inches / 10 centimeters. It shouldn't be too tightly knitted, just cozy! A little ribbing at the beginning and end makes the hat stretchy but strong.

FINISHED MEASUREMENTS: 14½ in / 37 cm long and 17¼ in / 44 cm circumference when laid flat

MATERIALS: CYCA #6 (super bulky/roving) Easy from Sandnes (100% wool, 55 yd/50 m / 50 g) OR Eskimo Mix from Drops (100% Wool, 54 yd / 49 m / 50 g)

YARN AMOUNT AND COLOR: 150 g Ochre or Gray-Brown for one hat

NEEDLES: U.S. size 10½ / 6.5 mm + U.S. size 8 / 5 mm, 3 dpn for ears

GAUGE: Approx. 11 sts in stockinette on larger needles = 4 in / 10 cm.

Adjust needle sizes to obtain correct gauge if necessary.

Bear Hat

- With larger needles, CO 54 sts. Join, being careful not to twist cast-on row; pm for beginning of rnd. Work 6 rnds of k2, p2 ribbing. Now continue in stockinette for 13½ in / 34 cm. End with 4 rnds k2, p2 ribbing.
- **Ears:** I placed the ears by measuring on Helmi to see where the ears should be. I put the tube flat on the table and measured 3¼ in / 8 cm in on the hat, 1 in / 2.5 cm in from the folded top. Each ear is 2 in / 5 cm wide at the base and the ears should be placed 2¾ in / 7 cm apart.
- With smaller needles, along the head, pick up and knit 8 sts with one dpn + 8 sts behind first set of sts with second dpn— these sts will form the outside and inside of the ear. Join to knit in the round.
- Knit 3 rnds.
- *K1, M1 (lift strand between two sts and knit into back loop) at each edge. It is important to increase with M1 because it will be almost invisible, whereas a yarnover will make a hole. Knit to last st on first ndl, M1, k1. Rep from * for back of ear.
- Knit 1 rnd.
- K1, M1, k2, p4, k2, M1, k1 on front.
- K1, M1, knit to last st and M1, k1 on back.
- K3, p6, k3 (front).
- K12 (back).
- Ssk, k2, p4, k2, k2tog (front).
- Decrease 1 st at each side of back: Ssk, k6, k2tog.
- Decrease the same way on every rnd until 4 sts rem.
- (Ssk, k2tog) 2 times = 2 + 2 sts rem.
- Cut yarn and draw through rem 4 sts; fasten off end. Weave in all ends neatly on WS. Block hat (see page 30).
- If you want to make the ears larger, you can add a few rows before you increase, increase to the total number of sts as above and then decrease on every other rnd instead of every rnd.
- Go out and wiggle those ears!

GARTER STITCH COWL WITH WAVY EDGING

Warm, soft, and easy to wear. Both sturdy and sheer, with a wavy edging to finish off the cowl nicely. Wear it on a crisp autumn evening with your favorite sweater or cardigan, or outside your winter coat. Wrap it around your neck if you are chilly, and let it slip down over your shoulders so the edging shows well.

FINISHED MEASUREMENTS: 7 in / 18 cm wide, 63 in / 160 cm long before finishing

MATERIALS: CYCA #4 (worsted/afghan/aran) Ullgarn Extra 2 from Yllet (95% wool/5% Merino wool, 219 yd/200 m / 100 g) + CYCA #0 (lace/fingering) Ullgarn Extra 1 from Yllet (100% wool–blend of Gotland pälsull and Falkland Merino, 437 yd/400 m / 100 g)

YARN AMOUNTS AND COLORS: 100 g Ullgarn Extra 2—Rye 312; 30 g Ullgarn Extra 1—Dark Gray 192

NEEDLES: U.S. size 8 / 5 mm: for cowl and U.S. size 2.5 / 3 mm for edging: circular at least 32 in / 80 cm long

GAUGE: 13 sts in garter st with larger needles and 2-ply yarn = 4 in / 10 cm.

20 sts in stockinette with smaller needles and 1-ply yarn = 4 in / 10 cm.

Adjust needle sizes to obtain correct gauge if necessary.

- With larger needles and Ullgarn Extra 2, CO 24 sts. Always begin each row with sl 1 purlwise. Work back and forth in garter st (knit every row) until piece is 63 in / 160 cm long. Twist the piece one full turn; place the ends edge to edge and sew them together. This method of joining allows the cowl to sit well on the shoulders.
- With smaller size circular and Ullgarn Extra 1, pick up and knit 300 sts along one edge of cowl. If necessary, pick up more or fewer stitches, in multiples of 10 sts (1 pattern repeat = 10 sts). It is very important that the total stitch count be a multiple of 10.
- Purl 1 rnd, knit 1 rnd, purl 1 rnd before beginning lace edging. Work charted rows once and then BO loosely.
- Weave in all ends neatly on WS and block cowl (see page 30). Pin out or stretch out the points as the cowl dries so that the edging will stand out.

Edging

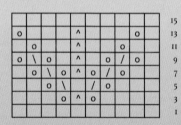

Work the edging following the chart. The even-numbered rows are not charted and all the sts should be knit around.

	knit on RS, purl on WS
o	yarnover
\	ssk
^	s2kp = sl 1 knitwise wyb, k2tog, psso
/	k2tog

ENTRELAC SCARF

Entrelac produces a knitted fabric that looks almost woven or braided. The garment is worked block by block. If you prefer, knit a shorter piece and sew the ends together to make a cowl (see page 62). The instructions here are for a piece that is not very wide but quite long. You can easily make the scarf wider by adding blocks. Each block is 8 sts wide. The technique will look especially good in a multi-color yarn as shown here. I have to warn you, though—entrelac can become quite addictive!

FINISHED MEASUREMENTS: 9 in / 23 cm wide, 79 in / 200 cm long

MATERIALS: CYCA #4 (worsted/afghan/aran) 2-ply space-dyed yarn from Hjelholts Uldspinderi (100% wool, 437 yd/400 m / 200 g)

YARN AMOUNT AND COLOR: 250 g Blue-Gray 03

NEEDLES: U.S. size 8 / 5 mm

GAUGE: Approx. 14 sts = 4 in / 10 cm. The gauge is not critical. The structure should be obvious but the blocks should not be knitted too tightly.

Adjust needle size to obtain correct gauge if necessary.

BASE TRIANGLES:
- CO 24 sts.
- *Row 1 (RS): K1; turn.
- Row 2 and all WS rows: Purl across.
- Row 3: Sl 1 purlwise wyb, k1; turn.
- Row 5: Sl 1 purlwise wyb, k2; turn.
- Row 7: Sl 1 purlwise wyb, k3; turn.
- Row 9: Sl 1 purlwise wyb, k4; turn.
- Row 11: Sl 1 purlwise wyb, k5; turn.
- Row 13: Sl 1 purlwise wyb, k6; turn.
- Row 15: Sl 1 purlwise wyb, k7; do not turn*
- Repeat from * to * until all the sts across have been worked.

TIER 1 (CONSISTS OF 1 LEFT TRIANGLE, 2 BLOCKS, AND 1 RIGHT TRIANGLE):

Left Triangle at side/Left Triangle:
- Row 1 (WS): K1; turn.
- Row 2: Kfb = 2 sts; turn.
- Row 3: Sl 1 purlwise, p2tog; turn.
- Row 4: P1, M1, k1; turn. It is important that you increase with M1 rather than a yarnover to avoid the hole that results from a yarnover.
- Row 5: P2, p2tog; turn.
- Row 6 and all following RS rows: Knit to the last st, M1, k1; turn.
- Row 7: P3, p2tog; turn.
- Row 9: P4, p2tog; turn.
- Row 11: P5, p2tog; turn.
- Row 13: P6, p2tog; turn.
- Row 15: P7, p2tog; do not turn = 8 sts in left triangle.

>

> **Blocks (make 3 alike):**
- **Row 1 (WS):** With WS facing, pick up and purl 8 sts along side of next triangle or block. Turn.
- **Row 2:** K8; turn.
- **Row 3:** Sl 1 purlwise, p6, p2tog; turn.
- **Rows 4–15:** Repeat the previous 2 rows 6 more times; at the end of Row 15, do not turn. After completing 3 blocks, work a right triangle as follows.

Right Triangle at side/Right Triangle:
- **Row 1 (WS):** With WS facing, pick up and purl 8 sts along side of next triangle or block. Turn.
- **Row 2 and all following RS rows:** Sl 1 purlwise, knit to end of row; turn.
- **Row 3:** Sl 1 purlwise, p5, k2tog; turn.
- **Row 5:** Sl 1 purlwise, p4, k2tog; turn.
- **Row 7:** Sl 1 purlwise, p3, k2tog; turn.
- **Row 9:** Sl 1 purlwise, p2, k2tog; turn.
- **Row 11:** Sl 1 purlwise, p1, k2tog; turn.
- **Row 13:** Sl 1 purlwise, k2tog; turn.
- **Row 15:** K2tog.
- The remaining st is counted as the first st to be picked up on the first block of the next tier.
- Turn work and move rem st to right needle.

TIER 2 (CONSISTS OF 3 BLOCKS)
- **Row 1 (RS):** With RS facing, pick up and knit 8 sts along the edge of the next block or triangle. On the first block use the rem st of previous tier as the first st to "pick up."
- **Row 2:** P8; turn.
- **Row 3:** Sl 1, k6, ssk.
- Repeat the previous 2 rows another 6 times; at the end of Row 15, do not turn. Repeat Rows 1–15 four more times (or more if you added extra sts); turn.
- Now repeat Tiers 1 and 2 until the scarf is as long as you like. Work Tier 1 once more before working the last tier with triangles.

FINAL TIER (TRIANGLES)
- **Row 1 (RS):** With RS facing, pick up and knit 8 sts along edge of next block or right triangle. The rem st of the previous tier counts as the first st to be picked up. **NOTE:** On following rows, slip the first st purlwise.
- **Row 2 and all following WS rows:** Purl across; turn.
- **Row 3:** K2tog, k5, ssk; turn.
- **Row 5:** K2tog, k4, ssk; turn.
- **Row 7:** K2tog, k3, ssk; turn.
- **Row 9:** K2tog, k2, ssk; turn.
- **Row 11:** K2tog, k1, ssk; turn.
- **Row 13:** K2tog, ssk; turn.
- **Row 15:** K2tog. The st remaining will be used as the first st of the next triangle.

- Work 3 triangles the same way. When all the triangles are complete, fasten off last st. Weave in all ends neatly on WS. Block scarf (see page 30).

ENTRELAC COWL

Here's a good project for learning entrelac or using up some leftover yarn—or both.

FINISHED MEASUREMENTS: 20½ in / 52 cm circumference, 11½ in / 29 cm wide

MATERIALS: CYCA #4 (worsted/afghan/aran) 2-ply space-dyed yarn from Hjelholts Uldspinderi (100% wool, 437 yd/400 m / 200 g)

YARN AMOUNT AND COLOR: 80 g Blue-Gray 03

NEEDLES: U.S. size 8 / 5 mm

GAUGE: Approx. 14 sts = 4 in / 10 cm. The gauge is not critical. The structure should be obvious but the blocks should not be knitted too tightly.

Adjust needle size to obtain correct gauge if necessary.

- CO 32 sts. Follow the instructions for the scarf on page 58 until the piece is approx. 9 in / 23 cm long. Keep in mind that there will be 1 more block on every tier because the cowl has 1 more 8-st repeat than the scarf. Work Tier 1 before you work the finishing tier. After completing all the triangles, fasten off and weave in all ends neatly on WS. Join the short ends.
- Block the cowl (see page 30).

Entrelac Cowl

HERMANNA'S COWL

A soft and lofty cowl or neck warmer with a pattern taken from Hermanna Stengård's collection. The motif is called "rose wreath" and is also found on traditional garments on the Faroe Islands and in Estonia.

SIZES: Child, 3–10 years (adult)

FINISHED MEASUREMENTS: 8¾ in / 22 cm (12¼ in / 31 cm) high; 9 in / 23 cm (10¾ in / 27 cm) wide

MATERIALS: CYCA #4 (worsted/afghan/aran) Ullgarn Extra 2 from Yllet (95% wool/5% Merino wool, 219 yd/200 m / 100 g) OR CYCA #4 (worsted/afghan/aran) 2-ply space-dyed yarn from Hjelholts Uldspinderi (100% wool, 219 yd/200 m / 100 g)

YARN AMOUNTS AND COLORS: MC: 30 (60) g Light Gray 01; CC: 20 (50) g Navy Blue 350

NEEDLES: U.S. size 9 / 5.5 mm

GAUGE: 17 sts = 4 in / 10 cm (an 8-stitch repeat = approx. 1¾ in / 4.5 cm.

Adjust needle size to obtain correct gauge if necessary.

- This cowl uses a space-dyed yarn for the main color (background) and a solid color yarn for the pattern (CC). With MC, CO 80 (104) sts. Join, being careful not to twist cast-on row; pm for beginning of rnd.
- Work 6 rnds of k1, p1 ribbing. Now work in pattern following the chart for 7 (9½) in / 18 (24) cm. Finish with 6 rnds k1, p1 ribbing.
- BO in ribbing at same tension as for cast-on row. Block cowl (see page 30).

Hermanna Stengård was born in Väskinde on Gotland in 1861. She was a teacher and also worked with handcrafts at the folk school in Roma. Following her interests, she began collecting old Gotland knitting patterns and garments. Her work was published in a book called Gotländsk sticksöm (Gotland Knitting) in 1925. The collection was later catalogued and is now preserved by Gotland's Handcraft Association. The collection has inspired many knitting designers and researchers. It has been spread widely in various ways through the years, not least through various knitting books about the Nordic and Scandinavian knitting traditions. Hermanna's own book has recently been reprinted—check the Resources at the back of this book to find out more.

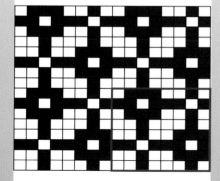

GRIMSLÄTT SCARF

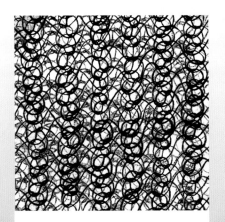

If you can't find the recommended lovely singles yarn for this scarf, try another similar fine yarn. The technique will look its absolute best with a singles yarn and large needles–the structure will show well and the shawl will be soft and supple. It will also be very warm because the loft is insulating. The technique is easy to knit but takes concentration.

FINISHED MEASUREMENTS:
10¾ x 69 in / 27 x 175 cm, unstretched

MATERIALS: CYCA #1 (sock/fingering/baby) Hand-dyed singles yarn from Grimslätt gård (100% wool, 459 yd/420 m / 100 g)

YARN AMOUNT AND COLOR:
100 g Blue

NEEDLES: U.S. size 10½-11 / 7 mm

GAUGE: It is difficult to give an exact gauge for this technique so use the measurements above as a guide. Begin with a gauge swatch so you can decide if the structure and texture of the pattern is obvious without being too open. You can also decide if you want to knit the scarf with or without edge sts.

Adjust needle size to obtain correct gauge if necessary.

- CO 21 sts as loosely as possible. The stitch count will be quadrupled over the next two rows. The first and last two stitches of every row are edge stitches—slip the first st of every row purlwise and knit all other edge sts.
- The instructions below are for the pattern motif only—the edge stitches are not included.
- **Row 1:** K1, (yo, k1) across.
- **Row 2:** K1, *insert needle from back to front of the yarnover of previous row and slip the yarnover, yo (= 1 new st), k1 (over knit st of previous row): rep * to * across.
- **Row 3:** K1, *insert the needle from back to front of the yarnover of previous row and slip the yarnover, yo, k2tog with the yarnover of previous row and 1 knit st*; rep from * to * across. = Slip the "hank," add a "hank," knit the "hank" and a knit stitch together (see below).
Repeat Row 3 until the scarf is desired length.
When it's time to bind off, work the bind-off over two rows as follows:
- **Bind-off Row 1:** Knit across without adding any new yarnovers.
- **Bind-off Row 2:** Bind off as usual, knitting each yarnover and treating each yarnover as a separate stitch so the edge will not pull in.
- Weave in all ends neatly on WS. Block shawl (see page 30). Make sure the edges are straight when you block the piece. Steam-pressing (under a damp pressing cloth) is also an excellent way to finish this shawl.

Slip the "hank," add a "hank," knit the "hank" and a knit stitch together. (A "hank" is an old Swedish term for a yarnover)

BOHUS WRIST WRAPS (REVLINGAR)

Traditional Bohus province wrist warmers are an excellent way to use up some leftover yarns. They are easy to knit and a good way to try out various knitting stitch techniques. These wraps are knitted in garter stitch, but why not try out brioche knitting, a ribbed pattern, seed stitch, or some other technique you'd like to sample? Just keep in mind that different stitches will require different amounts of yarn.

I knitted an I-cord to hold these wraps in place. Use the yarn amounts and measurements here as a general guide. Perhaps you'd like your "revlingar" to wrap a few times around your wrist? Calculate with your measuring tape and try it out!

FINISHED MEASUREMENTS:
3¼ in / 8 cm wide and 11¾ in / 30 cm long, excluding cord

MATERIALS: CYCA #1 (sock/fingering/baby) Ullgarn Extra 2 from Yllet (95% wool/ 5% Merino wool, 437 yd/ 400 m / 100 g)

YARN AMOUNT AND COLOR: 25 g Brown 60—small size

NEEDLES: U.S. size 2.5 / 3 mm for the wrap + U.S. size 1.5 / 2.5 mm for the I-cords: 2 dpn

GAUGE: 9 sts in garter stitch on larger needles = 1¾ in / 4.5 cm.

Adjust needle size to obtain correct gauge if necessary.

- With larger needles, CO 18 sts. Work back and forth in garter st (knit every row but purl the first st of every row) for 11½ in / 29 cm.
- Now shape the point: P1, ssk, knit until 3 sts rem, k2tog, k1. Decrease the same way on every other row until 4 sts rem. Knit all non-decrease rows. Next row: K1, k2tog, k1.
- The 3 sts remaining will be used for the I-cord.
- Change to smaller needles. *Do not turn work. K3, pulling in working yarn on WS. Slip the 3 sts back to tip of needle*; rep * to * until cord is 11¾ in / 30 cm long. BO the 3 sts.
- Weave in all ends neatly on WS.
- Block the wrist wraps (see page 30) and never suffer freezing wrists again!

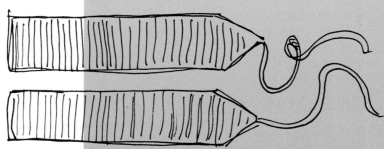

These wrist warmers are made as strips. They wrap around the wrist and are held in place with cords.

HIGHLAND COWL

Close, warm, and garter stitch knitted with narrow stripes of the simplest lace. It's perfect for under a jacket! Knit this cowl with the soft Highland wool as shown here or use similar size leftover yarns. Maybe you want to add more colors? If you want a scarf instead of a cowl, just make the piece 8–11¾ in / 20–30 cm longer than suggested below, so it'll be long enough to wrap comfortably around your neck. I sewed the ends together so the cowl will lie in place nicely.

FINISHED MEASUREMENTS: 8 in / 20 cm wide, 63 in / 160 cm long before seaming

MATERIALS: CYCA #1 (sock/fingering/baby) Highland Wool from Isager (100% wool, 306 yd/280 m / 50 g)

YARN AMOUNTS AND COLORS:
MC: 70 g Ocean
CC: 15 g Curry

NEEDLES: U.S. size 2.5 / 3 mm

GAUGE: 24 sts in garter st = 4 in / 10 cm.

Adjust needle size to obtain correct gauge if necessary.

- With MC, CO 48 sts. Work back and forth in garter st (knit every row but always purl the first st of each row). Knit 18 garter ridges—1 ridge = 2 knit rows. The ridges make it easy to count rows.
- Change to CC for the lace band and knit 2 rows (with the first row on RS). Now work an eyelet row as follows:
- P1, (yo, k2tog) across, end with k1.
- Knit 1 row on WS and then change back to MC.
- *Work 18 garter ridges with MC and then change to CC and work the 4 rows of lace band. Repeat from * until piece is 63 in / 160 cm long—or 13 times. End with a lace band.
- BO with MC. Weave in all ends neatly on WS and block cowl (see page 30). Twist the piece a full turn and then seam the short ends together.
- If you want to knit a scarf instead, end with a garter stitch section with MC.

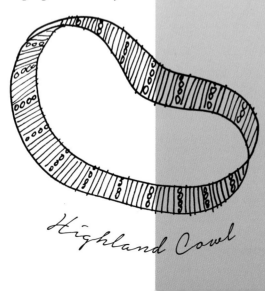

Highland Cowl

EVERYDAY MITTENS

Once upon a time, I bought a pair of Latvian mittens. They were the right size and had a lovely pattern in orange and light blue on a dark blue background. The cuff was very colorful and had a Latvian braid at the edge. There was something that attracted me to these mittens—and I found they fit well, even though, as typical for the Latvian and Estonian mitten traditions (as opposed to the Norwegian), they don't have thumb gussets.

I wore the mittens every day during the cold seasons. After my maternity leave, which involved both snow shoveling and many strolls with the baby carriage, the palms were so patched that there was more patching than original mitten. So it was time for a new pair of mittens with new colors and shaping. The main pattern from these favorite Latvian mittens migrated to the new pair.

The new mittens have a simpler, alternative thumb with a wave pattern, but I've included the chart for the original thumb motif in case you'd rather knit that for your mittens.

SIZE: Adult small

FINISHED MEASUREMENTS: 9¼ in / 23.5 cm total length; 4 in / 10 cm from base of thumb to edge of cuff; 8 in / 20 cm circumference of hand (measured with mitten flat)

MATERIALS: CYCA #1 (sock/fingering/baby) Finullgarn from Rauma (100% wool, 191 yd/175 m / 50 g)

YARN AMOUNTS AND COLORS:
15 g Ochre Yellow 4197 (A),
5 g Apricot 4206 (B),
10 g Black-Brown 410 (C),
10 g Sea Green 4887 (D),
30 g White-Gray 403 (E),
30 g Medium Gray 405 (F)

NEEDLES: U.S. size 0 and 1.5 / 2 and 2.5 mm: set of 5 dpn

GAUGE: 17 sts in pattern with larger needles = 2 in / 5 cm.

Adjust needle sizes to obtain correct gauge if necessary.

LATVIAN BRAID

• With smaller needles and Colors A and C, CO 72 sts as follows: With Color A over your index finger and C over your thumb, cast on with long-tail method so that Colors A and C alternate. Join, being careful not to twist cast-on row.
• **Rnd 1:** (K1 with A, k1 with C) around.
• **Rnd 2:** Bring both strands to the front—they will both stay on the front as you work around. (P1 with A, p1 with C) around, always bringing the color to be used next OVER the previous color. The strands will twist as you work, but try to slide the twist down the yarn because the strands will untwist as you work Rnd 3.
• **Rnd 3:** Bring both strands to the front—they will both stay on the front as you work around. (P1 with A, p1 with C) around, always bringing the color to be used next UNDER the previous color.

> • Change to larger needles and work the charted pattern.
> • When you reach the row outlined with red on the chart, place the 15 thumb sts on a holder and CO 15 new sts. This method of working the thumbhole (rather than working over waste yarn) will make it easier to pick up and knit sts later on and allows you to try on the mitten for fit.
> • Continue charted pattern.
> • Notice that at the top left side of the chart, there is a + symbol to indicate the beginning of the top shaping. I increased 1 st at this point between the two sides of the mitten to avoid the ugly "steps" which would otherwise appear.
> • Decrease with k2tog at left side and ssk at right side on each side of mitten = 4 sts decreased per round.
> • Shape top of mitten as shown on chart.
> • Cut yarn and draw through rem 9 sts and fasten off. Weave in all ends neatly on WS. Block mittens (see page 30). Two-color stranded knitting really benefits from wet blocking. After washing mittens, pin or pat out to finished measurements and lay flat to dry.

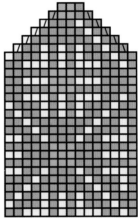

Left Thumb

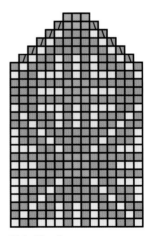

Right Thumb

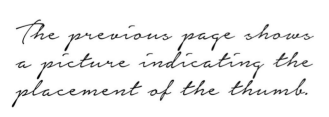
The previous page shows a picture indicating the placement of the thumb.

Chart for Everyday Mittens

If you want to make larger mittens, you can try going up a needle size, choosing a heavier yarn, or adding a pattern repeat. The risk is that the mittens will be too long and have the wrong proportions.

If you have trouble with the Latvian braid instructions, check YouTube.com for some help. It is absolutely worth the trouble to learn this technique.

HALF GLOVES

These are the best half gloves for everyday wear. The folded-up edge gives the illusion of layer on layer and makes the gloves beautifully warm. The singles yarn helps the glove fit the hand and provides a more tailored look. Why not try some variety with striping? The simple shaping invites so many options! I like to fold up the cuffs when I'm bicycling so that my wrists have total protection from the cold air. Wear yours as you like!

FINISHED MEASUREMENTS: 12¾ in / 32 cm total length; 6¾ in / 17 cm hand circumference (excluding thumb)

MATERIALS: CYCA #4 (worsted/afghan/aran) Ullgarn Extra 2 from Yllet (95% wool/5% Merino wool, 219 yd/200 m / 100 g) + CYCA #0 (lace/fingering) Ullgarn Extra 1 from Yllet (100% wool–blend of Gotland pälsull and Falkland Merino, 437 yd/400 m / 100 g)

YARN AMOUNTS AND COLORS: 50 g Ullgarn Extra 2 Gray 396 and 20 g Ullgarn Extra 1 Light Gray 196

NEEDLES: U.S. sizes 1 and 4 / 2.25 and 3.5 mm: sets of 5 dpn

GAUGE: 14 sts in stockinette with singles yarn and smaller needles = 4 in / 10 cm.

5 sts in ribbing with 2-ply yarn on larger needles = approx. 1½ in / 3.5 cm.

Adjust needle sizes to obtain correct gauge if necessary.

YOU'LL ALSO NEED: A needle and contrast color yarn or a stitch holder

- With larger needles and 2-ply yarn, CO 30 sts and divide sts onto dpn. Join, being careful not to twist cast-on row; pm for beginning of rnd.
- Work around in k3, p2 ribbing for 9¾ in / 25 cm. Pm about 1¼ in / 3 cm down from inner edge. BO in ribbing.
- Change to the smaller needles and, with singles yarn, pick up and knit 40 sts along cast-on edge.
- Divide sts with 10 sts each on 4 dpn and pm between Ndls 1 and 4. Work around in stockinette for 2¼ in / 5.5 cm.
- Begin thumb gusset: M1 between Ndls 1 and 4, k1, M1. I use the M1 method for increasing as it is almost invisible and avoids the hole which would be made by a yarnover.
- Knit 2 rnds. Increase as before with 3 sts between the increases. Knit 2 rnds.
- Increase as before with 5 sts between increases; knit 2 rnds. Continue shaping thumb gusset as set with 2 rnds between each increase rnd until there are 11 thumb gusset sts. Knit 2 rnds after final increase rnd.
- Place the 11 gusset sts on a holder. CO 5 sts over the gap and continue around in stockinette until the glove measures 4¼ in / 11 cm from the point where you picked up the 40 stitches around.
- Now work 5 rnds of k3, p2 ribbing. BO in ribbing.
- Pick up and knit sts for the thumb: knit the 11 sts from the holder, pick up and knit 3 sts up to the 5 cast-on sts; pick up and knit 5 sts and then 3 sts on opposite side of thumbhole = 22 sts total. Divide sts onto dpn and work around in stockinette for ¾ in / 2 cm. Now work 5 rnds k1, p1 ribbing.
- BO in ribbing. Weave in all ends neatly on WS. Block half gloves (see page 30).
- Make the second glove as for the first but begin the thumb gusset between Ndls 3 and 4.

Chimney Sweep
Hat and Point to
Point Shawl

CHIMNEY SWEEP HAT

A basic hat that is soft, warm, and lovely. Knit it striped or with a single color. Add a pompom to the top! It's easy to adjust the size so the hat can fit anyone.

If you want an upturned brim, work it in another form of ribbing, such as k2, p2 for 2 in / 5 cm. Knit a round where you want to fold up the hat and then reverse the ribbing, with knit over purl and vice versa. This way, the folded brim will blend into the rest of the hat. If you choose this option, begin the shaping sooner. Try on the hat to make sure the shaping works out. Maybe start at 7 in / 18 cm—and don't forget a folded brim means you'll need more yarn for the hat.

FINISHED MEASUREMENTS:
21¼–22¾ in / 54–58 cm head circumference; add or subtract sts in multiples of 5 for larger or smaller size.

MATERIALS: CYCA #4 (worsted/afghan/aran) Ullgarn Extra 2 from Yllet (95% wool/5% Merino wool, 219 yd/200 m / 100 g)

YARN AMOUNT AND COLOR: 50 g Gray 396

NEEDLES: U.S. size 4 / 3.5 mm: set of 5 dpn or short circular

GAUGE: 5 sts in semi-stretched 3/2 ribbing = approx. 1½ in / 3.5 cm.

Adjust needle size to obtain correct gauge if necessary.

- CO 80 sts and divide onto dpn. Join, being careful not to twist cast-on row. Pm for beginning of rnd. Work around in k3, p2 ribbing for 8¾ in / 22 cm (7½ in / 19 cm if you don't want a brim for the hat). Now begin the top shaping.
- **Decrease Rnd 1:** (K3, p2tog) around = 64 sts rem.
- **Next 2 rnds:** (K3, p1) around.
- **Decrease Rnd 2:** Sl 2 knitwise at the same time, k1, psso, p1) around = 32 sts rem.
- **Next 2 rnds:** (K1, p1) around.
- (Sl 2 sts through back loops, k1, psso. Sl 2 knitwise at the same time, p1, psso) around until 2 sts rem; k2tog tbl = 11 sts rem.
- Knit 1 rnd.
- Cut yarn and thread end into a tapestry needle. Draw yarn through rem sts, tighten and fasten off. Weave in all ends neatly on WS. Block hat (see page 30).

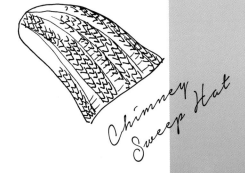

Chimney Sweep Hat

POINT-TO-POINT SHAWL

This accessory is somewhere between a shawl and a scarf. Garter stitch makes it very stretchy and supple. If you want to jazz it up, brightly colored tassels on each end will make it extra cheerful. Totally wearable for everyday and soft as a cloud of wool. The best kind of wool.

FINISHED MEASUREMENTS:
10¾ in / 27 cm wide at center, 61 in / 155 cm from point to point after blocking.

MATERIALS: CYCA #4 (worsted/afghan/aran) Ullgarn Extra 2 from Yllet (95% wool/5% Merino wool, 219 yd/200 m / 100 g)

YARN AMOUNT AND COLOR: 100 g Gray 398

NEEDLES: U.S. size 9 / 5.5 mm

GAUGE: 15 sts in garter st = 4 in / 10 cm.

Adjust needle size to obtain correct gauge if necessary.

- The scarf is worked entirely in garter st. Always slip the first st of every row purlwise.
- CO 3 sts.
- **Row 1:** K3.
- **Row 2:** Sl 1 purlwise, k1, M1, k1. It is important that you increase with M1 rather than a yarnover to avoid a hole.
*Knit 3 rows (don't forget to slip the first st of each row purlwise).
- **Increase Row:** Sl 1 purlwise, k1, M1, knit to end of row.*
- Repeat from * to * until there are 34 sts.
- Increase 6 more times with 5 knit rows between increase rows = 40 sts.
- Knit 5 rows after last increase row.
- ***Decrease Row:** Sl 1 purlwise, k1, k2tog, knit to end of row. Knit 5 rows*. Rep * to * until 34 sts rem.
- Now decrease as set on every 4th row until 3 sts rem.
- BO. Weave in all ends neatly on WS and block scarf (see page 30).
- You can embellish your scarf by adding a lace edging as described on page 57 or page 88, or, add color stripes in the garter stitch.

Point-to-Point Shawl

KNITTED SAW-TOOTH EDGING

Do you have a scarf that you've gotten tired of that needs a second chance? Maybe you want to liven up a pair of wrist warmers or a simple triangular shawl such as the linen one on page 49? This edging is a perennial favorite. It's easy and fun to knit. A shawl with a sawtooth edging immediately feels more finished. And the edging can be worked in a different yarn than used for the shawl or scarf!

- With RS facing, use a circular needle to pick up and knit sts along the entire edge. CO 4 new sts to begin the sawtooth edge. The first row will be the WS.
- **WS:** K3, p2tog with the last edging st and next st picked on garment edge. Turn.
- **RS:** Sl 1 knitwise with yarn behind and work Row 1 (see below). Turn and continue with Row 2, etc:

- **NOTE:** Always slip the first st knitwise wyb.
- **Row 1:** Sl 1, k1, yo, k2.
- **Rows 2, 4, 6:** Sl 1, k to last st, p2tog (joining edging and shawl sts).
- **Row 3:** Sl 1, k2, yo, k2.
- **Row 5:** Sl 1, k1, yo, k2tog, yo, k2.
- **Row 7:** Sl 1, k2, yo, k2tog, yo, k2.
- **Row 8:** BO 4 sts knitwise and knit to end of row (including join of edging and edge sts).
- Repeat Rows 1–8.
- BO. Weave in all ends neatly on WS. Block completed garment (see page 30) or gently steam-press only the edging.

Row 8

Row 7

Row 6

Row 5

Row 4

Row 3

Row 2

Row 1

| V | sl 1 knitwise with yarn held behind |

| □ | knit on RS, purl on WS |

| o | yarnover |

| / | k2tog |

| + | p2tog joining last st of edging to 1 st from garment edge |

| — | BO 4 sts knitwise. |

Single-color balls, spotted balls, and multi-color balls in shades that either contrast with or blend in tone with each other. It's fun to try out color combinations on pompoms. Try it yourself!

POMPOMS AND TASSELS

A simple and fun way to change the look of almost any garment. Even small bits of leftover yarns work here. Don't be afraid to blend different yarn weights or fibers—but do it sensibly. The classic chimney sweep hat on page 86 looks great with a pompom, while the point-to-point shawl on page 87 has tassels at each point. Take a look at page 96 for more ideas. If you get tired of the pompoms or tassels, all you have to do is untie them or cut them off.

MATERIALS: Leftover yarns

YOU'LL ALSO NEED: Card stock or cardboard, a pen, measuring tape, scissors

POMPOMS—PERHAPS YOU HAVEN'T MADE ONE SINCE YOU WERE A CHILD?

• Measure the diameter of the pompom you want. Draw two circles, the same diameter, on the card-stock or cardboard. Make a smaller circle inside each large circle (see Drawing 1). I think ⅝ in / 1.5 cm is a good measurement for the area to wrap the yarn around. Cut out the center of each circle. Now it's time to wrap the yarn around the circles while they are held together (see Drawing 2). It's easier if you thread the yarn through a tapestry needle. Try to wind evenly so that your pompom will be as even as possible (see Drawing 3).

• How much yarn you want is a matter of taste. The more yarn, the tighter the pompom. When you've finished wrapping, cut a doubled length of strong thread about 15¾ in / 40 cm long. Make sure the thread is strong enough to hold the yarn once you've cut it. The thread will be inserted between the two circles when you cut the yarn off them.

>

> • Pull the yarn down a little from the edges of the circles so you can insert the scissor points between the circles. Carefully cut the yarn all around (see Drawing 4). Now wrap the doubled thread around the yarn between the circles and tie it firmly (see Drawing 5). Finish by cutting the circles away and discarding them. Trim the ball evenly.

• You can buy pompom makers in various sizes. These can be reused. Sometimes it's a little harder to wrap the yarn around the plastic pompom makers because the yarn might slide before you can cut it. Try one out—and remember that practice makes perfect!

• Do you want to make a spotted pompom? Alternate wrapping a single-color (main color) yarn with a contrast color. The contrast color will provide the spots; make each spot 3-5 strands wide and then wrap 10 strands of the main color before adding another spot.

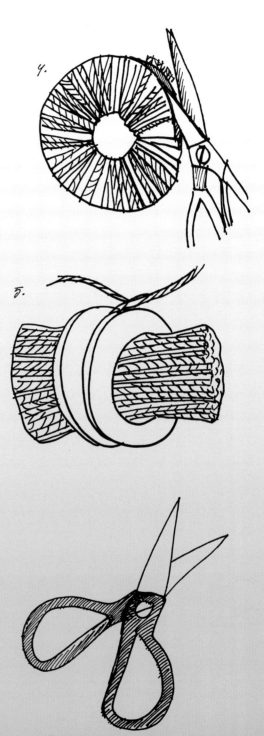

4.

5.

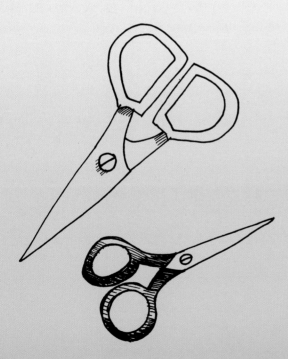

94

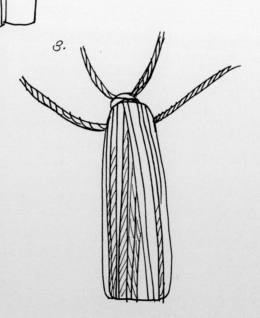

1.

2.

TASSELS—EASY TO MAKE AND THEY LOOK SO GREAT!

• Measure the desired length for the tassel. Cut a bit of cardstock or cardboard the same length and at least 2 in / 5 cm wide. Wrap the yarn around the template (see Drawing 1). The amount of yarn to wind depends on how full you want the tassel to be and the proportion of volume to length. A thick tassel should be longer than a thin one so it will have a balanced shape. When you've finished wrapping, cut a length of strong thread about 15¾ in / 40 cm long. Thread it into a tapestry needle and slide it under the yarn at the top of the template. Tie a couple of knots to secure the tassel (see Drawing 2).

• Insert the scissors into the lower edge of the template and cut the tassel open. Cut another strand of thread or yarn about 12 in / 30 cm long. Remove the template and wrap the thread/yarn around, slightly below the top of the tassel (see Drawing 3). Fasten off the wrapping thread (you can hide the end inside the tassel). Trim the tassel evenly and adjust the top wrap as needed (see Drawing 4).

3.

4.

YARN

Yarn is half the experience, if not more, of knitting and wearing knitted garments. I hope that you will try some new yarns and squeeze the skeins a little extra the next time you are choosing yarn. Think about what you want to use the yarn for and what you want for the materials. How are the strands plied? How tightly was the yarn spun? Does the garment need to be durable or soft? Think about color, shape, and how you want the garment to drape and feel. It will be a pleasant journey of discovery!

ISAGER

has sold quality yarns in delightful fiber and color selections since 1977. Since then, Marianne Isager, who founded the company, has been considered one of the foremost Danish and Scandinavian knitting designers. Some of the yarns Isager still sells today have been sold since the beginning. www.knitisager.com

GRIMSLÄTT GÅRD

is run by Sara and Marcus Toreld. Their farm is primarily for raising Gotland sheep. During the summers, the sheep graze on the salt meadows in Fjällbacka's archipelago and the Tjurpanna's nature reserve outside Grebbestad. The sunshine and the salt and minerals that the sheep eat help produce a very soft and lustrous wool. The Torelds sell fleeces, skins, and meat through distributors. www.grimslatt.se.

HJELHOLTS ULSPINDERI

located on the island of Fyn in Denmark, was established in 1887. The mill has many years experience spinning the wool of Nordic landrace sheep, producing fine and even yarns. Sheep owners can leave the fleeces from their sheep at the mill and have it processed and spun for their own yarn. The mill's color shifting yarns are nice to work with—they have the luster of Gotland wool and softness of Falkland Merino. Merino sheep fare well on the Falkland Islands and the Merino wool from the islands is considered more ethically desirable than Merino from other areas. www.hjelholt.dk.

YLLET FURNISHING

is run by Frida Asplund in Visby on the island of Gotland. At the shop, you can buy Yllet's yarn that has been produced since 1982 with the softest Swedish Gotland and Falkland Island Merino wools. Three yarn qualities are spun and dyed at Hjelholt's Mill in Denmark. The lustrous linen yarns, which have been spun almost as far back, are available in lovely colors. The linen yarns are dyed at Holma Helsingland in Hälsingland, Sweden. The linen yarns bear the "Good Environmental Choice" label. www.ylletinredning.se.

SOLKUSTENS SPINNVERKSTAD

is a mill in Roslagen near Norrtälje, run by Ingrid Danielsson and Fredrik Dickfelt. Anyone who has their own sheep can leave the wool here and have it spun on antique machinery from Scotland. The mill also produces its own line of yarns with Swedish wool in natural sheep's wool colors. They spin singles, two- and three-ply yarns. Each skein is saturated with knowledge, care, and love for the sheep, handcrafts, and materials. www.solkustens-spinnverkstad.com.

RAUMA ULLVAREFABRIKK

produces one of my absolutely favorite yarns: Rauma Finullgarn! It's nearly unbeatable for mittens. Available in a wealth of colors, it's easy to knit with, and just gets better and better as the garments are worn. Soft but still distinct stitches. This yarn is excellent for two-color stranded knitting! www.theyarnguys.com or www.nordic-fiberarts.com in the U.S. (www.raumaull.no).

ÖSTERGÖTLANDS ULLSPINERI

is based in Storeryd, Sweden and spins its own assortment of yarns, including Visjö which is a favorite for many knitters. It is a soft, easy-to-knit Finnsheep wool yarn available in many fine colors. The wool is carefully selected and spun on a traditional Spinning Jenny with roots in the 1700's. The mill is run by Ulla-Karin and Börje Hellsten. www.ullspinneriet.com.

MARKS & KATTENS

is a well-established company that sells various types of yarn for knitting, patterns, and embroidery materials. I have used their Eco Wool that is spun with 100% organic wool, according to its statements. The seven different natural shades are soft, single-ply and rather loosely spun. www.marks-kattens.se

SANDNES GARN

is a Norwegian company that has supplied yarn for both hand knitting and industry since the end of the nineteenth century. They sell a large variety of yarns. www.sandnesgarn.no.

DROPS

has, since the beginning of the 1980s, produced and sold a large assortment of yarns and patterns. Eskimo is one of their basic yarns. It is a natural yarn that is easy to knit with and very suitable for felting. It's also excellent for the Bear Hats on page 54. www.garnstudio.com.

RESOURCES AND INSPIRATION

BOOKS:

Albright, Barbara. *The Natural Knitter: How to Choose, Use, and Knit Natural Fibers from Alpaca to Yak*. New York: Potter Craft, 2007.

Bergdahl, Violet and Ella Skoglund. *Gotländsk sticksöm* [Knitting from Gotland]. Stockholm, Sweden: LTs förlag, 1983.

Bush, Nancy. *Knitted Lace of Estonia: Techniques, Patterns, and Traditions*. Loveland, CO: Interweave, 2008.

Bonniers stora bok om stickning [Bonniers' Big Book of Knitting]. Stockholm, Sweden: Bonniers, 2006.

Engquist, Ulla. *Sticka—Detaljer som gör skillnad*. Stockholm, Sweden: Hemslöjdens förlag, 2015. English edition forthcoming in 2016 as Knitting Details Start to Finish from Trafalgar Square Books.

Falk, Clara and Kamilla Svanlund. *Vantar för alla årstider* [Mittens for Every Season]. Göteborg, Sweden: Andina, 2013.

Gottfridsson, Inger and Ingrid Gottfridsson. *The Swedish Mitten Book: Traditional Patterns from Gotland*. Asheville, NC: Lark Books, 1984.

Gustafsson, Kerstin and Alan Waller. *Ull* [Wool]. Stockholm, Sweden: LTs förlag, 1987. [last name misspelled in Swedish edition]

Isager, Helga. *Finstickat* [FineKnitting]. Stockholm, Sweden: Natur och Kultur, 2012. (Some patterns from the collection are available in English on ravelry.com.)

Lind, Vibeke. *Knitting in the Nordic Tradition*. Asheville, NC: Lark Books, 1984.

Pagoldh, Susanne. *Nordic Knitting: Thirty-One Patterns in the Scandinavian Tradition*. Loveland, CO: Interweave, 1991.

Stengård, Hermanna. *Gotländsk sticksöm: Gamla mönster* [Knitting from Gotland: Old Patterns]. Bromma, Sweden: Rediviva, 2014 (reprint of original 1925 edition).

Trotzig, Eva and Erika Åberg. *Varmt och stickat* [Warm and Knitted]. Sundbyberg, Sweden, 2013.

Wiklund, Signild. *Textil Materiallära* [Textile Material Lessons]. Stockholm, Sweden: LTs förlag, 1984.

WEB PAGES:

Knitty, an online magazine: www.knitty.com

Ravelry, a forum for knitters: www.ravelry.com

BLOGS:

Asplund Knits: asplundknits.blogspot.se

Clara Stickar: clarastickar.blogspot.se

Dödergok: dodergok.blogspot.se

En till stickblogg: entill.typepad.com

Handarbetaren: handarbetaren.com

Kate Davies: katedaviesdesigns.com

Knitbot: knitbot.com

Magasin Duett: magasinduett.blogspot.se

Maria Carlander: mariacarlander.blogspot.se

Med pinner: pinnehobby.blogspot.com

Stickigt: sticky.typepad.com

Tant Kofta: tantkofta.blogspot.se

Viffla, now Clara Linnea: claralinnea.se

FIND ME AT:

Crafts by Wynja: www.wynjacraft.blogspot.com.

THANK YOU TO

Malin Nuhma for taking the fine photos, the poetry, the magic, and because we had so much fun while working. Thanks!

Eva Bergman for excellent editing and feedback—you do it so well!

Anja Larsson for the layout which came out exactly as it should have.

Annelie Lindqvist and the publisher because I got to write a book!

Heléne Wallin because you made such clear charts and helped me to knit.

Eva Svensson, Annika Hedling and Annkristin Hult for invaluable knitting help.

Malin Göthberg because you hustled around the island with us and modeled in the sun, rain, and storms.

Maria Hultberg because we got to borrow you and Berså for coffee breaks, photography, and beauty.

Jenny Őrjestad, Christine Kilefors, Esmeralda, Elvira, Helmi, Ny Björn and Valdar because you worked as models for the book.

Birgitta Rasmusson and Benny Rondahl because we got to meet, photograph, and learn more about alpacas, sheep, and pygmy goats.

Helmi, Valdar and Ny Björn because you are everything to me.

Katarina, Marian, Eva, Malin, Frida, and many others because you thought about and answered countless questions—"Is it soft enough? It is comfortable? Should I change the color?"

All my comrades in knitting and crafts. There couldn't be any better friendship.

A big thank you,
Erika